HOW WILL IT GET THERE?

Jo Cleland

Rourke
Publishing LLC
Vero Beach, Florida 32964

www.rourkepublishing.com

PHOTO CREDITS: page 4: © Corel; page 5: © Rey Rojo; page 6: © Furchin; page 8: © Sharon Meredith; page 9: © Bojan Tezak; page 10: © Slobo Mitic; page 11: © Image 100; page 12: © Bonnie Jacobs; page 17: © Sigrid Albert; page 18: © Elena Koreubaum; page 19: © Mary R. Vogt; page 20: © Jade; page 21: © Andreas Steinbach; page 22: © Electricspace

Editor: Robert Stengard-Olliges

Cover design by Nicola Stratford

Library of Congress Cataloging-in-Publication Data

Cleland, Jo.
  How will it get there? / Jo Cleland.
     p. cm. -- (The world around me)
  ISBN 1-59515-989-4 (Hardcover)
  ISBN 1-59515-960-6 (Paperback)

Printed in the USA

CG/CG

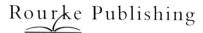

Rourke Publishing

www.rourkepublishing.com – sales@rourkepublishing.com
Post Office Box 3328, Vero Beach, FL 32964

TABLE OF CONTENTS

Honk, honk! Toot! Beep! Where are all these noisy **vehicles** going and what are they carrying?

TRAINS AND PLANES

Look at the tools. How will they get to the workers?

A train will take them there.

Look at the letters. How will they get to our friends?

A plane will take them there.

SUBWAYS AND BUSES

Look at the people. How will they get to work?

The **subway** will take them there.

Look at the children. How will they get to school?

The big yellow bus will take them there.

VANS AND BICYCLES

Look at the pretty flowers. How will they get to the **hospital**?

A van will take them there.

Look at the sandwiches. How will they get to the people in time for lunch?

A bicycle will take them there.

FERRIES, TRAILERS AND TRACTORS

Look at the cars. How will they cross the water?

The ferry boat will carry them across.

Look at the horses. How will they get to the fair?

A trailer will take them there

Look at the **hay**. How will it get to the horses?

A tractor will get it there.

Glossary

hay (HAY) — grass or other plants cut and dried for food for animals

hospital (HOSS pi tuhl) — a place where sick or injured people go for medical care

subway (SUHB way) — an underground railroad in a city

vehicle (VEE uh kuhl) — anything made for carrying passengers, animals, goods, or equipment

Index

Further Reading

Francis, Dorothy. *Our Transportation Systems*. Millbrook Press, 2002.
Loves, June. *Bicycles and Motorcycles*. Chelsea House Publishers, 2002.
Stille, Darlene. *Freight Trains*. Compass Point Books, 2002.

Websites To Visit

http://www.roadway.com/kids/trucks.html
http://www.boeing.com/companyoffices/aboutus/kids/

About The Author

Jo Cleland, Professor Emeritus of Reading Education, taught in public education and at the College of Education at Arizona State University West. Jo continues to work with children through her storytelling and workshops. She has presented to audiences of teachers across the nation and the world, bringing to all her favorite message: *What we learn with delight, we never forget.*